READY, SET, NOVEL!

A WRITER'S WORKBOOK
PLAN AND PLOT YOUR UPCOMING MASTERPIECE

By Chris Baty, Lindsey Grant, and Tavia Stewart-Streit

of National Novel Writing Month

ISBN: 978-1-4521-0-1729

Manufactured in China

Designed by Parallel-Play

10 9 8 7 6 5 4 3 2 1

Chronicle Books LLC
680 Second Street
San Francisco, California 94107
www.chroniclebooks.com

CONTENTS

INTRODUCTION

YOU ARE HERE!

Hi and welcome! We're so glad you made it. We were just hanging out and chatting with your new novel. Have you met your book yet? Really interesting! Great storyteller! And good-looking too!

You've clearly got a winner on your hands, and we're excited to spend the next month helping you two get to know each other a little better. As part of that process, we'll take field trips, block out opening scenes, stalk some characters, brainstorm intriguing twists, draw maps, and forge a majestic plot cannon that will launch you headlong into novel-land. By the time you've filled this journal, you and your novel will have a complete blueprint for your new life together.

You'll also have a very nicely colored picture of Fyodor Dostoyevsky.

WE'RE RIGHT HERE WITH YOU

As the organizers of National Novel Writing Month, we write alongside our 200,000 participants, spending November savoring the joys and challenges of penning a 50,000-word novel in thirty days. Among the three of us, we've written seventeen reasonably unhorrible novels, and we've been lucky enough to help thousands of people get books written. We don't claim to know everything about writing fiction, but we have spent a lot of time learning what works and what doesn't when it comes to novel prep.

This workbook contains all the battle-tested activities, prompts, and bits of creative mayhem that have helped us (and our friends) enjoy many productive months of noveling abandon. Don't yet know what you want to write about? *Ready, Set, Novel!* will help you figure it out. And if you already have a handle on your plot, we'll work with you to firm up your arcs, flesh out your characters, and discover new aspects of your story.

You can unleash the power of *Ready, Set, Novel!* in many different ways. Dip into it sporadically for quick bursts of inspiration, plow through it methodically from start to finish, or just get your writing courage up by slapping the High-Five Hand on page 114 for a few hours. This is an anything-goes kind of workbook. If you work best with deadlines (and we love deadlines!), consider rolling through the entire workbook during the course of one action-packed month, like so:

ACTION-PACKED MONTH

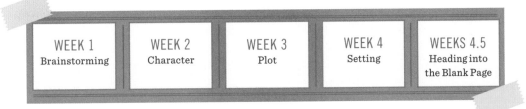

| WEEK 1 | WEEK 2 | WEEK 3 | WEEK 4 | WEEKS 4.5 |
| Brainstorming | Character | Plot | Setting | Heading into the Blank Page |

Whatever your time frame, novel planning works best when you let it be messy. Think of *Ready, Set, Novel!* as a test kitchen. Your job now is to strap on the apron and safety goggles and throw a lot of things against the wall to see what sticks.

In the context of this workbook, that means covering these pretty pages with a lot of ink. Whatever you do, don't get caught up in the soul-sucking, productivity-hindering idea that you need to be 100 percent confident of a character detail or bit of prose before you add it to the journal. Just write it! If it turns out not to be quite right, you can always cross it out and try again. No one will read this except you, so dive into the writing exercises, lists, and questionnaires with wordy abandon, even if it feels a little awkward at first.

To help you get into the right mind-set, we have a quick activity for you. (Yes, we know it's not fair to ask you to do things when you haven't even gotten out of the introduction yet. But we're bossy that way. And this activity is important!)

It's called Fill This Box with Crap. And the task is, you guessed it, to completely fill this box. With crap. Write anything you like. Make a to-do list from your pet's point of view. Draw your best friend's left nostril. Catalog the last five things you ate, and then rank them. Shake ink from your pen and make Rorschach blots by folding the page in half. All that matters is that you fill up the box. Ready? Go to it.

OK? You're done? It's completely filled? Are you already cringing a little at some of the stuff that ended up in there?

That's A-OK. Just by throwing all that stuff onto the page, you've already taken the first step in spatula-ing yourself off the griddle of self-criticism and flipping yourself up into more creative realms. Remember: Your novel will grow richer with every bit of ink, crayon, or paint you feed the workbook. Half-baked thoughts, weird notions, doodles, bad ideas that you scratch out later—they all belong here.

And now, with your sleeves rolled up and some ink (or paint) on your fingers, our literary adventure together can really begin. Stormy brain, ahoy!

CHAPTER ONE

Storming Your Brain

Activity Checklist

- [ ] The Love List
- [ ] Pull Your Novel Out of a Hat
- [ ] The What-If Game
- [ ] Your Tale's Tone
- [ ] Literary Dish Washing
- [ ] Surfing the Inspiration Superhighway

We've got some good news and some bad news about your novel.

The good news is that, whether you realize it or not, you already have a ton of great material for your book. The juicy, hilarious, heartbreaking ideas that will eventually form the core of your novel are all around you now. They're hiding in conversations among your coworkers, they're stuffed into your favorite songs, and they're tucked into the machinations of the questionable reality TV show you watched last night. Some great ideas even stow away inside bad ideas—their brilliance becoming clear only when you work off the gunk concealing the genius.

Now for the bad news. You won't be able to fit every great idea or interesting scenario you come up with during these next few weeks into a single story. Your job in this chapter is twofold: to churn out great amounts of noveling fodder and then to cherry-pick the most intriguing ideas to blend up into a story. Happily, this is fun, inspiring work. In fact, some writers love the brainstorming phase so much that they forget to actually write the book they've spent years planning. This will not be your problem.

As you work through this section to find new book ideas—or supplement ones you've already cooked up—there are three things to keep in mind.

1. **Ideas are like celebrities.** They're unstable, they're attention hogs, and they never do their share of the laundry. On the plus side, they're also highly sociable—once you get a couple, others will show up to keep them company. Ponder your book whenever you have a free moment, and know that once you get an intriguing notion or two to show up at your brainstorming party, the entourage won't be far behind.

2. **Document everything.** Fill the Playground at the back of this journal with every creative spark the moment it occurs to you, no matter how small it seems or how confident you are that you'll remember it later. Every writer is tormented by the unforgettable plot twist she ended up forgetting. Also, be sure to jot down interesting notions, even if you're sure they won't fit into your current novel. If they don't fit in the story you're writing now, they may be perfect for its sequel.

3. **Two stormy brains are better than one.** Whether you have a few scattered ideas or a fullfledged plot, share what you've got with a friend, and then brainstorm some possible big-picture story directions together. (If you end up using some of his suggestions, you can take him out for a thank-you dinner on your yacht when your first royalty check comes in.)

A special note for bookish overachievers: Even if you already have your plot, setting, characters, and tone mostly worked out, you'll likely find something in this chapter that helps add a few layers to your story. If you have your entire story locked down, though, you can skip the exercises that follow and go straight to the Playground, where we'd like you to write out a loose synopsis of your book, as if you were walking a friend through each section. When you're done, read it over and underline or highlight areas that need fleshing out. Then meet us in Chapter Two (page 20), where we'll begin filling in some of those holes by getting to know your protagonist a little better.

THE LOVE LIST

To kick off this brainstorming session, make a list of places and things that excite, inspire, or intrigue you. Examples are: cooking, particle physics, fonts, 1940s Los Angeles, dreams, ghosts, running, guitars, knitting, prehistory, aliens, science, family, romance/relationships, small towns, dogs, tango dancing, and road trips.

NOW
Circle at least nine things on the list that you would be excited about putting in your novel. Congratulations! Your book has begun. Go to the next page to find out what the heck we're talking about.

The things that you're drawn to in life are the subjects that you'll wield well as a writer. For our next trick, we're going to ask the universe to hand you three possible novels for which you'd be the perfect author.

STEP 1 ·

Write down your nine favorite circled items from the Love List (page 12) on separate scraps of paper.

STEP 2 ·

Dump the scraps into a hat or coffee cup.

STEP 3 ·

Pull out three scraps of paper. Jot down the three elements you picked on the Novel 1 note card to the right. Go back to the hat again and pull out three more scraps; these go on the Novel 2 note card. The remaining three scraps go on the Novel 3 note card.

NOW Look over your noveling note cards, and mull over your three options. Do any of these combinations of place and personal passions sound intriguing? Grab the best ones, and turn the page to flesh them out in the What-If Game (page 14).

Or, if the universe dealt you a bum hand, forget the hat, and just pick three or more of your favorite Love List items that might play well together.

NOVEL 1

SCRAP 1:

SCRAP 2:

SCRAP 3:

NOVEL 2

SCRAP 1:

SCRAP 2:

SCRAP 3:

NOVEL 3

SCRAP 1:

SCRAP 2:

SCRAP 3:

THE
WHAT-IF
GAME

 ACTIVITY

Thinking up interesting scenarios and exploring the stories that might unfold from them is a great way to kick-start a book. To play this brainstorming game, take your favorite story ideas from the previous activity and increase the intrigue by building some what-ifs around it. Example: What if a woman finally met Mr. Right . . . on her honeymoon? What if every inhabitant in a small town woke up one morning and discovered they'd all had the same dream about dancing the tango? What if DNA advances allowed scientists to bring a village of Neanderthals to life?

YOUR TALE'S TONE

To help you start thinking about the tone, storytelling style, and genre of your book, look through this list and check all the items that resonate with you.

- [ ] First-person point of view
- [ ] Third-person point of view
- [ ] Action-packed plot
- [ ] Slower-moving character study
- [ ] Happy ending
- [ ] Sad ending
- [ ] Sci-fi
- [ ] Romance
- [ ] Fantasy
- [ ] Literary fiction
- [ ] Experimental fiction
- [ ] Historical fiction
- [ ] Young adult fiction
- [ ] Spiritual

- [ ] Mystery
- [ ] Crime
- [ ] Paranormal
- [ ] Humorous
- [ ] Past tense
- [ ] Present tense
- [ ] Dialogue-heavy
- [ ] Straightforward timeline
- [ ] Nonlinear timeline
- [ ] Cliffhanger chapter endings
- [ ] Short chapters
- [ ] Long chapters
- [ ] Serial novel
- [ ] Novel made up of connected short stories

If we've missed anything, add it in yourself!

- [ ] _____
- [ ] _____
- [ ] _____
- [ ] _____
- [ ] _____
- [ ] _____
- [ ] _____

- [ ] _____
- [ ] _____
- [ ] _____
- [ ] _____
- [ ] _____
- [ ] _____
- [ ] _____

NOW Keep these checked boxes in mind as you begin shaping your story. Again, if you love it, you'll be a natural at writing it.

One of the strange things that thousands of National Novel Writing Month participants discover each year is that the richest book material often pops into your head while you're doing routine things like working out, showering, driving, washing dishes, or going for a walk. It's not clear why it works, but for some reason having your body engaged in a simple activity gives you access to the fertile parts of your imagination. List the top three activities that help your mind wander, then do each of them while you ponder your new novel.

· ·

TIP: Every novelist loses the thread of his story at some point (or points!) during the writing process. Revisit the routines you listed below anytime you get lost in novel-land.

ACTIVITY 1

ACTIVITY 2

ACTIVITY 3

NOW
Lock in any great thoughts you had while washing your literary dishes here.

If you're still looking for inspiration for your story, the Internet has an unbeatable array of sites rich with novel-worthy nuggets; secrets are revealed, new possibilities are glimpsed, and lives are changed. Here are a few types of sites we scour when searching for book ideas. As you visit sites, jot down any great novel ideas that spark up.

ONLINE POLICE BLOTTERS

If you're writing a mystery novel, detective story, or a page-turning thriller and are short on felonies, try doing an online search for "police blotter" or "crime log." These public records of the dramas unfolding around all of us will give you plenty of fodder for your book. (For a lighter take on the criminal element, look for police blotters published in small-town newspapers, which tend to be a less-bloody cornucopia of conflicts, rivalries, and misunderstandings.) And if your thriller needs some outright comic relief, check out the myriad of "weird news" sites on the web (newsoftheweird.com is a classic), which offer a cavalcade of inept criminals and priceless human-interest tales.

PUBLIC CONFESSIONALS

PostSecret (postsecret.com) is a public art project in which people submit their deepest, darkest secrets to be posted anonymously online. Browse through the postcards on the site (or do an online image search for "postsecret" for hundreds more), and make a note of secrets that could serve as suitable engines for your characters. In the same vein as PostSecret, Smith Magazine (smithmag.net) solicits six-word memoirs and publishes them online. The longing, humor, regret, and triumph in these true-life micro tales are powerful literary mojo.

INSPIRATIONAL NOTES

1,000 WORDS

From disasters in family togetherness (awkwardfamilyphotos.com) to the candid moments captured on the streets of the world (in-public.com), photography sites are a showcase for serendipitous moments when hidden truths rise to the surface. News services like Reuters (reuters.com) put together a gallery of each year's best photos, and browsing these striking images—especially if you skip the captions and imagine your own backstories for the photos—can help ideas bubble to the surface.

CHAPTER TWO

Creating Your Characters

Activity Checklist

- [ ] Freewriting About a Favorite
- [ ] Freewriting About Real-Life Characters
- [ ] Character Profiling
- [ ] Juicy Details
- [ ] Collaging Your Character
- [ ] Character Field Trip

- [ ] Character Lifeline
- [ ] Your Character Through the Ages
- [ ] Family Tree
- [ ] Family Dynamics
- [ ] Character Conversation
- [ ] Motivation Magic

It's character time! Now that you've broken the seal on your workbook and discovered what you'd like to write about, it's time to turn your thoughts to whom you'd like to write about. You may be thinking, "Do I have to do this?"

WHY YOU HAVE TO DO THIS

When you're in the wasteland between your plot idea and your actual plot, it's your characters who keep you company. They inspire you to keep writing and to keep fighting toward resolving their needs and wants. Put quite simply, your characters will get you there.

If you don't pay a shred of attention to anything else written here, these are the three things we think you should know about creating characters:

1. **Don't be shy.** At this stage, the more characters, the merrier. They may not all end up in your novel. In fact, you may harvest the best of each and create a Franken-character. But whatever you do, don't limit your imagination in creating a vast roster of characters.

2. **Get detailed. Get really detailed.** As if you were a cop, and the perp were a detail, tell him you're gonna take him down to Chinatown. That's how detailed. The nuances, quirks, and history you attribute to your characters will infuse them with dimension and—whether they're losers, heroes, or hiss-worthy villains—relatability.

3. **Find the motivation.** Not your own motivation (though you'll need some too) but that of your primary characters. What gets them out of the bed in the morning and allows them to sleep at night? What is the one thing each one wants more than anything else in the world? Find that, and you've got yourself a story!

MEETING YOUR CHARACTERS

The activities in this chapter will have your characters talking your ear off. They'll be revealing their hot-button issues and private passions, demonstrating their best and worst sides, and guiding you through the minutiae of their lives. You'll collage their loves and hates, climb inside their minds, and uncover truths only their therapists would know. By the time it is all over, you'll have observed your characters in their natural habitats—be it the classroom, construction site, or zoo. By writing them inside and out, you'll create the most realistic, fleshed-out, complex characters possible—characters who jump off the page, characters who will berate you, inspire you, and tell you that no, those jeans don't make you look fat. Aces, right? We know. Keep reading.

REWINDING YOUR CHARACTERS

Where your characters come from and what happened to them way back when can tell you volumes about their present selves. Determining who your main character's stepsister's great-grand-pappy was might shed some light on his passion for yurts. In this chapter, you'll also figure out what your main character was like as a baby (super-smart? colicky?), in kindergarten (a bed wetter? an adventurer?), in elementary school (spelling-bee champ? class clown?), in high school (drama queen, flunky, thrill-seeker, teenage lothario?), and in college (entrepreneur, dreamer, drug addict, recluse?). This trip down memory lane will leave you with a rich history for your main character.

SO NOW WHAT?

Turn the page and get to know the people (or beasts or aliens) who will populate your novel and keep you company while you're writing it. Time's a-wastin'!

FREEWRITING ABOUT A FAVORITE

Take a few minutes to write about your favorite character from a novel. What is the character like, and what about that do you particularly like? What are the character's flaws, and what makes him or her likable in spite of those faults?

Think about someone you know or see regularly who is completely over the top: a real-life "character." Write about the characteristics—both physical and behavioral—that make this person fascinating. Then invent a backstory that explains why this individual looks and acts the way he or she does. Feel free to do this for multiple real-life characters.

Fill out these character profiles for as many or as few of the players in your story as you like.

Name

Nickname

Age   Birth Date

M ☐   F ☐   Race/Ethnicity

Location

Profession

Education

Hobbies and Interests

Political and/or Religious Beliefs

Disposition and Personality

Name

Nickname

Age   Birth Date

M ☐ F ☐ Race/Ethnicity

Location

Profession

Education

Hobbies and Interests

Political and/or Religious Beliefs

Disposition and Personality

Name

Nickname

Age _____ Birth Date

M ☐ F ☐ Race/Ethnicity

Location

Profession

Education

Hobbies and Interests

Political and/or Religious Beliefs

Disposition and Personality

Name

Nickname

Age   Birth Date

M ☐ F ☐ Race/Ethnicity

Location

Profession

Education

Hobbies and Interests

Political and/or Religious Beliefs

Disposition and Personality

KEEP
GOING

Name

Nickname

Age   Birth Date

M ☐   F ☐   Race/Ethnicity

Location

Profession

Education

Hobbies and Interests

Political and/or Religious Beliefs

Disposition and Personality

Name

Nickname

Age   Birth Date

M ☐   F ☐   Race/Ethnicity

Location

Profession

Education

Hobbies and Interests

Political and/or Religious Beliefs

Disposition and Personality

KEEP GOING

Name

Nickname

Age   Birth Date

M ☐   F ☐   Race/Ethnicity

Location

Profession

Education

Hobbies and Interests

Political and/or Religious Beliefs

Disposition and Personality

Name

Nickname

Age   Birth Date

M ☐   F ☐   Race/Ethnicity

Location

Profession

Education

Hobbies and Interests

Political and/or Religious Beliefs

Disposition and Personality

KEEP
GOING

Name

Nickname

Age   **Birth Date**

M ☐   F ☐   **Race/Ethnicity**

Location

Profession

Education

Hobbies and Interests

Political and/or Religious Beliefs

Disposition and Personality

Name

Nickname

Age   Birth Date

M ☐ F ☐ Race/Ethnicity

Location

Profession

Education

Hobbies and Interests

Political and/or Religious Beliefs

Disposition and Personality

KEEP
GOING

JUICY DETAILS ACTIVITY

From your cast of characters in the previous activity, pick three that you feel especially drawn to and want to write more about. One will become your main character. The others may play an important role in your story (think sidekick, love interest, or nemesis!). Use these pages to delve deeper into the lives of your main and secondary characters.

CHARACTER NAME: _____

WEAKNESSES/FAULTS

PET PEEVES

FEARS

GUILTY PLEASURES

PRIZED POSSESSIONS

BAD HABITS

PROUDEST ACCOMPLISHMENTS

SECRET TALENTS

CHARACTER NAME: _____

WEAKNESSES/FAULTS

PET PEEVES

FEARS

GUILTY PLEASURES

PRIZED POSSESSIONS

BAD HABITS

PROUDEST ACCOMPLISHMENTS

SECRET TALENTS

KEEP GOING

CHARACTER NAME: _____

WEAKNESSES/FAULTS

PET PEEVES

FEARS

GUILTY PLEASURES

PRIZED POSSESSIONS

BAD HABITS

PROUDEST ACCOMPLISHMENTS

SECRET TALENTS

NOW Pick one of these people to be your main character. It's time to explore his or her past, present, and future!

Drawing from any resources at your disposal (magazines, bits of nature, fabric, paint, nail polish, stickers, stencils), create a collage that evokes your main character in some way: loves, hates, desires, style, hobbies, and/or worldview.

CHARACTER FIELD TRIP

 ACTIVITY

Go out into the real world and find your main character's doppelganger in his or her natural habitat. Write about the person's clothing, hairstyle, and accessories, and the way he or she walks and talks, the words he or she uses, and how he or she interacts with the people around him or her.

NATURAL HABITAT

_____

_____

_____

_____

_____

_____

_____

_____

_____

_____

_____

CLOTHING/APPEARANCE

_____

_____

_____

_____

_____

_____

_____

_____

_____

_____

_____

PHYSICAL MANNERISMS

_____

_____

_____

_____

_____

_____

_____

_____

_____

_____

_____

DIALOGUE/INTERACTIONS

_____

_____

_____

_____

_____

_____

_____

_____

_____

_____

_____

CHARACTER LIFELINE

Use this timeline to cover as many of your main character's milestones as you can. Go from birth all the way to death or from birth to the start of the novel, or just lay out key events from one very important year.

THE LIFE OF

Write two scenes featuring one of your characters at any of these stages of life: as a baby, in kindergarten, in elementary school, in high school, in college, or anytime before your novel begins. Or write scenes from one of the milestones listed in the lifeline you just completed.

SCENE 1: STAGE OF LIFE/MILESTONE FOR

_____

_____

_____

_____

_____

_____

_____

_____

_____

_____

_____

_____

_____

_____

_____

_____

_____

_____

_____

_____

_____

_____

_____

_____

_____

_____

SCENE 2: STAGE OF LIFE/MILESTONE FOR

FAMILY TREE ACTIVITY

Understanding your main character can be easier if you know his family history.
When filling out the family tree, feel free to add as many branches as you like!

NAME:

Profession: _____

Place of Birth: _____

Date of Birth: _____

NAME:

Profession: _____

Place of Birth: _____

Date of Birth: _____

NAME:

Profession: _____

Place of Birth: _____

Date of Birth: _____

NAME:

Profession: _____

Place of Birth: _____

Date of Birth: _____

NAME:

Profession: _____

Place of Birth: _____

Date of Birth: _____

NAME:

Profession: _____

Place of Birth: _____

Date of Birth: _____

NAME:

Profession: _____

Place of Birth: _____

Date of Birth: _____

NAME:

Profession: _____

Place of Birth: _____

Date of Birth: _____

NAME:

Profession: _____

Place of Birth: _____

Date of Birth: _____

NAME:

Profession: _____

Place of Birth: _____

Date Of Birth: _____

NAME:

Profession: _____

Place of Birth: _____

Date of Birth: _____

NAME:

Profession: _____

Place of Birth: _____

Date of Birth: _____

NAME:

Profession: _____

Place of Birth: _____

Date of Birth: _____

NAME:

Profession: _____

Place of Birth: _____

Date of Birth: _____

NAME:

Profession: _____

Place of Birth: _____

Date of Birth: _____

NAME:

Profession: _____

Place of Birth: _____

Date of Birth: _____

NAME:

Profession: _____

Place of Birth: _____

Date of Birth: _____

NAME:

Profession: _____

Place of Birth: _____

Date of Birth: _____

NAME:

Profession: _____

Place of Birth: _____

Date of Birth: _____

NAME:

Profession: _____

Place of Birth: _____

Date Of Birth: _____

FAMILY DYNAMICS

Describe the relationship between your main character and his immediate family. Include details about his home life and what makes this family who they are. (Are they nudists, for example, or a military family?)

How has the family dynamic shaped who your main character is now? Is there something he wants from his family but still hasn't gotten?

CHARACTER CONVERSATION

Use any of the following scenarios (or create your own) to write dialogue between your main character and any of your secondary characters:

- BREAKING A NEW YEAR'S RESOLUTION
- HAVING A DIFFICULT PHONE CALL WITH A PARENT
- ENDING A RELATIONSHIP
- ENCOUNTERING A FALLEN CHILDHOOD HERO
- GETTING ADVICE ON A DIFFICULT ISSUE OR PERSONAL CHALLENGE

You can write about these topics as they're happening, or write a conversation in which the characters rehash the incident.

Whether this dialogue makes it into your novel or not, it may shed some light on your main character's needs . . . and wants.

MOTIVATION MAGIC

ACTIVITY

Now that you've spent time with your main character and you know him inside and out, make a list of his wants and needs. Go big—no desire is too inconsequential.

WANTS

NEEDS

Looking at this list, figure out the single thing your character wants more than anything else (love, justice, forgiveness?), and write it in the magical box below.

 With this crucial bit of information about your character, you are ready to enter the realm of plot!

CHAPTER THREE

Plotting Your Story

Activity Checklist

- [ ] Your Real-Life Conflict
- [ ] Your Main Character's Conflict
- [ ] The Villain
- [ ] Light the Fuse
- [ ] Plot Your Problems
- [ ] The Plot Machine

- [ ] The Time Machine
- [ ] The Other Side
- [ ] Stuffing More Characters into the Cannon
- [ ] The Subplot Machine
- [ ] The Core
- [ ] The Pitch
- [ ] Plot Bits from the Universe

Congratulations on creating a solid cast of complex characters. You've chosen your lead and developed a couple sidekicks, and you have a small army of extras ready and willing to step in at your command.

Now it's time to figure out what all your new imaginary friends, foes, and frenemies are going to do in your novel. If reading that last line makes your palms sweat a little (or a lot) you are not alone. For 99 percent of the writerly population, the concept of getting characters from page one to The End is as daunting as the idea of flying a handmade dirigible across the Atlantic Ocean. But we've got good news: Plotting your novel is going to be far easier (and less dangerous) than you think. You may not believe us now, but by the end of this chapter, you'll have an intriguing story line, a masterful character arc, and a plot outline that will practically write your book for you.

THE FIVE SECRET STEPS TO STORY BUILDING

Once you have these steps down, you'll be churning out books faster than Krispy Kreme churns out hot doughnuts.

1. **Construct the cannon.** At the end of the previous chapter, you answered the question "What does your main character want more than anything else?" This question is so important that you'll be answering it for all of your characters, including your villain. This will give you enough subplots for a trilogy! Whether it's true love, sweet revenge, or a cupcake-filled swimming pool, a character's greatest desire is the cannon that propels her toward her destiny.

2. **Build the mountain.** If you want to write a book people will actually read instead of use as a face pillow, you're going to have to inflict some pain on the character you've just grown to love. Create conflict, suspense, and heart-wrenching drama by stacking a mountain of setbacks (fears, weaknesses, villains, spider monkeys) in front of your protagonist. That way, when your protagonist finally does find the person, planet, or swimming pool of her dreams, it will be so much more satisfying!

3. **Light the fuse.** Like you or me, your main character is a creature of habit. In order to start him on his quest, you'll need to literally light a fire beneath him. This event ignites the fuse on your character's cannon; it's the phone call from an old lover, the tragic loss, the trip to Vegas. It's what makes it impossible for your main character to continue in his old ways.

4. **Plot the problems.** Conflict is the fuel that moves your plot forward. And we are not talking about just one big blowout at your climax. Exciting plots have characters encountering problems right from the get-go. Think of the last comedy you saw. We bet our bottom dollar that the main character had to cleverly get himself out of one pickle after another until he had to wiggle his way out of the there's-no-way-he's-going-to-get-himself-out-of-this-pickle pickle at the climax of the film. The same should go for your book. Creating mini-problems to build up to the mega-problem is the best way to keep readers reading.

5. **Meet him or her on the other side.** The person that you load into the cannon at the start of your novel will be much different from the person you meet at the end, after she's reached the other side of the mountain. At the beginning, your protagonist may be a sad and reclusive computer nerd, but after saving the world from a nuclear holocaust, she becomes a confident vixen. How your main character changes in your book might not be as simplistic as nerd to superhero, but it's important that he or she does change and that your readers see the transformation unfold along the course of your novel.

FROM PLOTLESSNESS TO PLOTOPIA

If you're still feeling woozy about diving into this chapter, repeat this mantra: "I can totally do this." Now say it again. And again. And again.

You can!

Each activity in this chapter builds on the next, so take it one step at a time, maybe with a power nap (or a cup of strong coffee) in between. These activities build upon the five secret steps you just read about, helping you outline your plot, and—because supporting characters are people too—we'll provide space for you to map out a couple of their subplots.

After you've planned and plotted to your heart's content, we'll help you dig to the core of your novel: the single most important thing you want your reader to take away from it. Once you find this, you'll have everything you need to craft a compelling story that will endure the test of time . . . or at least keep you writing to the end.

Good luck, mighty writer, and most important, have fun!

Freewrite about what you yourself want more than anything else in the world (to become a best-selling author, find true love, open a petting zoo) and what (or who) is preventing you from getting it.

YOUR MAIN CHARACTER'S CONFLICT

ACTIVITY

Look back to page 53 where you wrote what your main character wants more than anything else in the world. This is your character's cannon: the thing that will propel him to do all the things you have in store for him. Rewrite this extremely important character factoid in the cannon below.

Write down all the things that will potentially block your main character. Is it her current romantic partner? A terminal illness? His battle with kleptomania?

. . . .

TIP: Look back at this character's greatest weaknesses and faults in the Juicy Details activity (page 34) before you begin writing. As you may have noted in the previous activity, internal struggles (fears, bad habits) are just as difficult to overcome as external ones (an oppressive political regime, many dragons).

THE VILLAIN ACTIVITY

You may have already listed this evil entity in Chapter Two, but now it's time to delve deeper into the mind of the villain. Your villain may be a living, breathing person, or he may be intangible (racism or poverty) or internal (insecurity or shyness). No matter what form your villain takes, he will represent the largest hurdle your protagonist needs to overcome in order to reach her goal.

Just like your main character, your villain has his own desires and will face his own setbacks. Answer the questions that follow.

What is your villain's greatest desire? Is it the same thing that your main character wants (to get the girl) or is it something different (to destroy the world)?

_____

_____

_____

_____

_____

_____

_____

_____

_____

What is in the way of the villain getting what he wants?

_____

_____

_____

_____

_____

_____

_____

_____

_____

_____

Write a scene describing your main character's first encounter with the villain.

LIGHT THE FUSE

Make a list of possible life-changing events that could light your story's fuse. Think in extremes: a shocking discovery, tragic news, or a once-in-a-lifetime opportunity. Write as many scenarios as it takes to find the one that will make it impossible for your main character to continue living life as she knows it.

SCENARIO 1

SCENARIO 2

SCENARIO 3

SCENARIO 4

SCENARIO 5

SCENARIO 6

Choose one of the scenarios and expand it into a scene in your novel.

PLOT YOUR PROBLEMS

ACTIVITY

The journey to the climax of your novel will be filled with mini-conflicts. List up to ten problems that your main character will need to solve before the mega-conflict or climax.

MINI-CONFLICTS

1.

2.

3.

4.

5.

6.

7.

8.

9.

10.

Write a potential climax.

_____
_____
_____
_____
_____
_____
_____
_____
_____
_____
_____
_____
_____
_____
_____
_____
_____
_____
_____
_____
_____
_____
_____
_____
_____

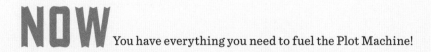 **NOW** You have everything you need to fuel the Plot Machine!

To make plotting your story as painless as possible, we've created the Plot Machine. This machine runs on Post-it notes, so grab a pack before you dive in. Once you have them, write each major event in your novel on a Post-it and arrange the notes along the Plot Machine to your liking. Start by placing the Post-its containing your beginning, climax, and ending events, but after that it's up to you. You can work backward, start at the beginning and post chronologically, or stick Post-its on the page randomly with your eyes closed.

. . . .

TIP: Not all plots follow this formula. Some begin with the climax or work backward from the resolution to the beginning. Experiment with the plot you just created by thinking beyond the traditional structure.

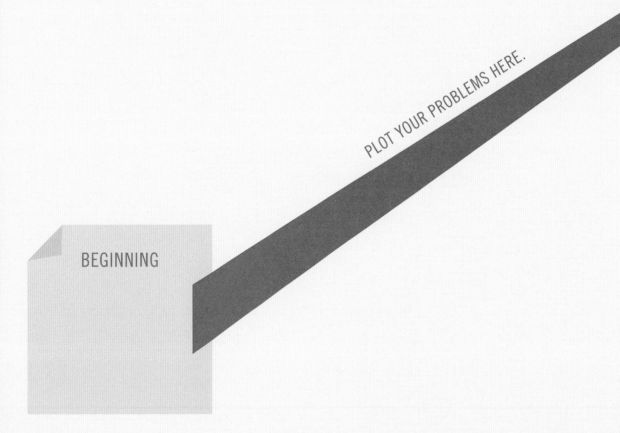

PLOT YOUR PROBLEMS HERE.

BEGINNING

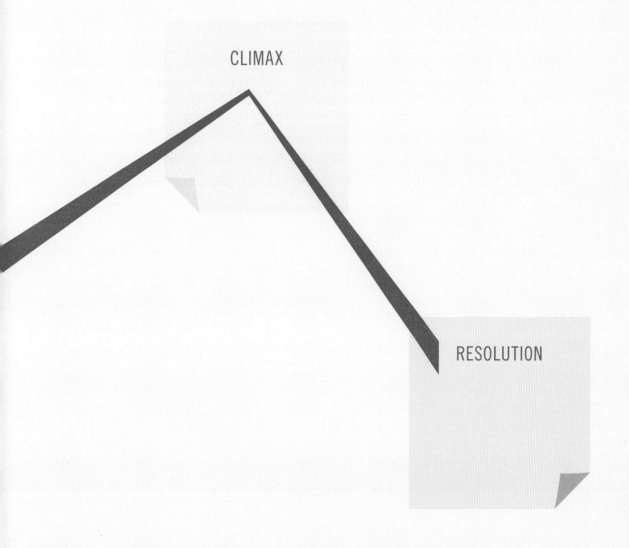

CLIMAX

RESOLUTION

NOW You have the events of your plot; it's time to get organized. Though you may know what will happen in your plot, you may not know *when* each thing will happen. The following timeline will help you arrange the events from the Plot Machine in order and within the time frame you'll be writing about them in.

THE TIME MACHINE

ACTIVITY

Once you've arranged the Post-its on the Plot Machine (pages 66–67) to your liking, use this time-line to lay out your novel. When doing this activity, consider the following: Does your novel take place during the course of a lifetime, a few years, or a day? Will your story unfold chronologically, or will you mix up the order of events? If you use flashbacks, where in the story will they go?

TIP: We suggest you use a pencil, just in case you change your mind about the order of events!

TIMELINE

TIMELINE

THE OTHER SIDE

In the Before column, list the traits that define your main character now (wimpy, a compulsive liar, works for an evil corporation). In the After column, define your character at the end of your book (brave, honest, sold everything to start a nonprofit).

TIP: Remember these changes don't need to be as straightforward as the examples we list. A wimpy character may be just as wimpy at the end but be more accepting of his timid ways.

BEFORE

AFTER

Write an "after" conversation between your main character and a secondary character that shows how he or she has changed by the end of your book.

Look back at the cast you created in the previous chapter (pages 24 to 34) and choose two supporting characters. These should be friends of the main character, not foes. Their job is to support your main character as he struggles to make his dreams come true. Write the names of these characters in the spaces provided, and then answer the following questions for each:

SUPPORTING CHARACTER 1: _____

In which ways will this character help the protagonist overcome the mountain of obstacles in store for him?

_____
_____
_____
_____
_____
_____
_____
_____
_____
_____
_____
_____
_____
_____
_____
_____
_____
_____
_____
_____
_____
_____

What does this supporting character want more than anything else?

What setbacks will block this character from getting what he wants?

KEEP
GOING

SUPPORTING CHARACTER 2: _____

In which ways will this character help the protagonist overcome the mountain of obstacles in store for him?

_____

_____

_____

_____

_____

_____

_____

_____

_____

_____

_____

_____

_____

_____

_____

_____

_____

_____

What does this supporting character want more than anything else?

_____

_____

_____

_____

_____

_____

_____

_____

_____

_____

_____

_____

What setbacks will block this character from getting what he wants?

_____

_____

_____

_____

_____

_____

_____

_____

_____

_____

_____

_____

_____

_____

THE SUBPLOT MACHINE

If you need subplots, grab some multicolored Post-it notes and look to your supporting characters. Their quests to get what they want more than anything else (which may be completely separate from the main character's quest) are the stuff that subplots are made of. Lay out subplots for each of your supporting characters (and even your villain) on the Subplot Machine using a different color Post-it note for each additional character.

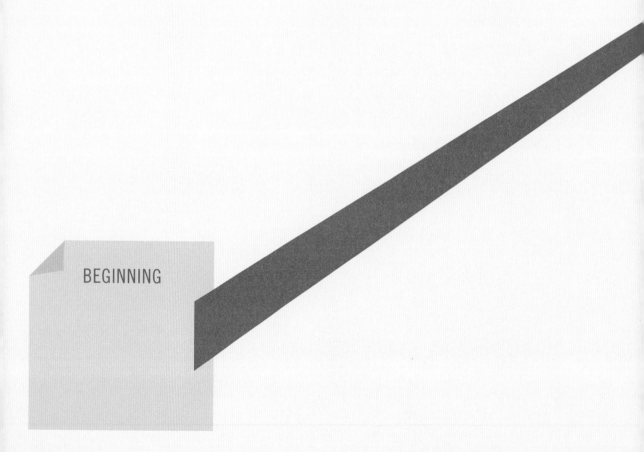

BEGINNING

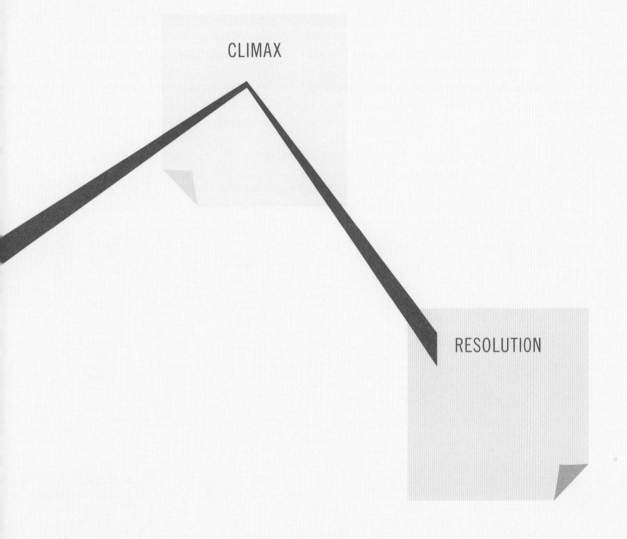

CLIMAX

RESOLUTION

NOW Let's dig into the core of your novel!

THE CORE

If your plot is what *happens* in your novel, the core is what it all *means*. This can be anything from "people can change" to "aliens are jerks." It's your book's lifeblood. It will give your novel cohesion and help you get back on track if you get lost while noveling. Think of it as your novel's thesis—just like when you're writing a paper, you never want to lose sight of this core concept while you work. Spend a little time freewriting about your core. Once you feel like you've found it, write a short version of it on a Post-it and place it in the frame.

. . . .

TIP: We know you might change your mind about your novel's core as you go. You may start the novel with "love is a pile of crap" but halfway through discover that "love conquers all" is actually closer to what you're writing about. Feel free to swap in a new Post-it anytime your core changes.

NOW
Copy this core onto another Post-it and stick it on your computer screen, so you never lose sight of it while you write.

Another great way to get a handle on your story is by writing a one-sentence summary of your plot. And not just any sentence. This is the action-packed, heart-wrenching, or laugh-out-loud sentence you'll use to blow the minds of literary agents and editors. Your pitch can include any or all of the following: your characters, the inciting incident, your setting, even elements of your core.

SAMPLE PITCH

An out-of-work physicist and a heartbroken artist find that love may be the only thing that can save the imploding universe.

PITCH

While planning your novel, you may come across hilarious photos, weird fortune cookie messages, or oddball business cards that you're not quite sure how to use in your book. This workbook comes with a built-in Plot Bits from the Universe storage space. You will find it behind the back cover. Save your discoveries in this pocket for a rainy day when you're out of writerly fuel and need a little inspiration.

CHAPTER FOUR

Exploring Your Setting

Activity Checklist

- ☐ Your Life, Your Setting
- ☐ The Guided Tour
- ☐ Sensing Your Setting
- ☐ Making a Map
- ☐ A Day in the Life
- ☐ Setting: Before & After

You've figured out your characters and what they're doing in your novel. Well done, writer! Before you go any further, take a moment to celebrate the magic you're making. Pat yourself on the back, have a Swiss Cake Roll, or sing a bar of "We Are the Champions."

Go on! We'll wait.

Good. Now that you've acknowledged your awesome accomplishments so far, we can get to the next exciting element of your novel: the setting.

If your brain is feeling a little squishy after all of the character creation and plot doctoring, we have some great news: Setting does a ton of work for you. Think of the setting as a super-hero with very specialized superpowers that can show your readers elements of the novel that might otherwise be missed and save you loads of writing time.

SETTING TO THE RESCUE!

How can one piddly element of your novel do so much, you might be asking? Sit back, relax, and read up on all the ways that setting works for you.

1. **Setting reinforces the mood of your novel.** In the plot section, you worked out what your main character is like in the beginning of the novel (broke, lonely, in danger) and where he'll be by the end (successful, fulfilled, dead). The mood of the story mirrors this trajectory, and the setting is the fastest and easiest way to convey this information. You don't need to write that your character feels frightened and vulnerable if you toss in a flickering street lamp and some dead leaves skittering across the deserted blacktop. And in the end, when your character has sent his enemies packing, his sense of security will be reflected in the well-lit streets with couples out walking their dogs and the pleasant hum of dinnertime conversation drifting from the open windows of the houses on his block.

2. **Setting gives your characters and their lives even more depth.** A main character living on a manicured cul-de-sac behind a wrought iron gate guarded by a 24-hour gatekeeper goes a long way toward explaining her compulsive tendencies and xenophobic anxieties. Compare this to her next-door neighbor and best friend, a free spirit who feels stifled by the cookie-cutter nature of her surroundings. Let your characters' immediate environments—and how they feel about them—do the work of telling your reader who these people are.

3. **Setting grounds the story in reality.** Whether the setting of your story is urban or rural, densely populated or nearly uninhabited, jungle-hot, torrentially rainy, crime-ridden, revolution-struck, sitting on the lip of an active volcano, or located in a galaxy far, far away, it provides the context for what happens to your characters and gives their day-to-day lives dimensionality and believability. Knowing that your main character sleeps under a mosquito net every night because the tropical climate is a breeding ground for malarial mosquitoes or that the villain is frequently impeded in his evildoing by the snowsuit he has to wear in the subzero wasteland he inhabits goes a long way toward bringing your story to life for the reader.

Cool, huh? And really, really helpful.

The activities in this chapter will have you pondering why your characters live where they do, how they feel about the place, and what effect this setting and the place in time has on the characters' day-to-day lives. Did they grow up there or move there for a job, a love interest, or because their chronic asthma required a different climate? Do they shop at Whole Foods or Grocery Outlet? Do they ride the bus to work, or does their driver drop them off in a town car? All of these details and more await your attention in the superpowerful lair that is the setting.

Freewrite about your relationship to where you live. How did you end up there? Are you happy with where you are? How does your current location affect your life? (Do you have to drive long distances, milk your cows, or use rain barrels?)

_____

_____

_____

_____

_____

_____

_____

_____

_____

_____

_____

_____

_____

_____

_____

_____

_____

_____

_____

_____

_____

_____

_____

_____

_____

_____

_____

_____

_____

_____

_____

_____

_____

_____

_____

_____

_____

_____

_____

_____

_____

_____

_____

_____

_____

_____

_____

_____

_____

_____

_____

_____

_____

NOW

Keeping the connection between your life and where you live in mind, let's look at your novel's setting.

THE GUIDED TOUR

Take a moment to establish the big-picture when-and-where of your novel. (Are we in suburban America in 1954? Normandy during WWII? The planet Meegrob in 2090?) Within the larger setting of your novel, where do your characters live? Writing in the voices of your main and supporting characters, give the reader a tour of their neighborhoods. Have them describe what their neighborhoods look like, what they love and hate about where they live, and why they're there.

MAIN CHARACTER GUIDED TOUR

KEEP
GOING

SUPPORTING CHARACTER 1 GUIDED TOUR

CHARACTER NAME: _____

_____
_____
_____
_____
_____
_____
_____
_____
_____
_____
_____
_____
_____
_____
_____
_____
_____
_____
_____
_____
_____
_____
_____
_____
_____
_____
_____

SUPPORTING CHARACTER 2 GUIDED TOUR

CHARACTER NAME: _____

_____

_____

_____

_____

_____

_____

_____

_____

_____

_____

_____

_____

_____

_____

_____

_____

_____

_____

_____

_____

_____

_____

_____

_____

SENSING YOUR SETTING

 ACTIVITY

Write a scene about your main character in one of his favorite—or least favorite—spots by incorporating what he sees, hears, smells, feels, and, if possible, tastes there.

TIP: For inspiration, visit some places similar to locations in your novel. If you're writing about a historical, futuristic, or otherwise-invented setting, take an armchair field trip.

Use this blank map to plot the world that your characters inhabit. Draw it yourself or paste in pieces of other maps; whatever works for you!

TIP: Study existing maps or take a tour of your own neighborhood and note landmarks and locations you could include.

	1	2	3	4	5	6	7	8	9
A									
B									
C									
D									
E									
F									
G									
H									
I									

LEGEND

	11	12	13	14	15	16	17	18	19	
										A
										B
										C
										D
										E
										F
										G
										H
										I
	11	12	13	14	15	16	17	18	19	

A DAY IN THE LIFE

Fill in these day planners for three of your characters, from the moment they wake up in the morning to the end of the day. (What time do they get up? How long are their showers? Or do they go to the gym before work? Do they work? Where, and at what times?)

THIS DAY BELONGS TO:	
7:00	4:00
8:00	5:00
9:00	6:00
10:00	7:00
11:00	8:00
12:00	9:00
1:00	10:00
2:00	11:00
3:00	12:00

Pick one thing from this character's daily life and write a scene about the character in that place, including any internal or external dialogue that the place prompts.

KEEP
GOING

7:00	4:00
8:00	5:00
9:00	6:00
10:00	7:00
11:00	8:00
12:00	9:00
1:00	10:00
2:00	11:00
3:00	12:00

Pick one thing from this character's daily life and write a scene about the character in that place, including any internal or external dialogue that the place prompts.

KEEP
GOING

THIS DAY BELONGS TO:

7:00   4:00

8:00   5:00

9:00   6:00

10:00   7:00

11:00   8:00

12:00   9:00

1:00   10:00

2:00   11:00

3:00   12:00

Pick one thing from this character's daily life and write a scene about the character in that place, including any internal or external dialogue that the place prompts.

_____

_____

_____

_____

_____

_____

_____

_____

_____

_____

_____

_____

_____

_____

_____

_____

_____

_____

_____

_____

_____

_____

_____

_____

_____

KEEP
GOING

SETTING: BEFORE & AFTER

Is your novel suspenseful, lighthearted, or adventure-filled? Write a scene that highlights the mood of your novel in the beginning of the story, using details about the setting that you've established throughout this chapter.

TIP: Before anything dramatic happens, most stories begin with a description of a character in a place. The scene you write here could be the first page of your novel.

If the mood of your novel changes from beginning to end, write about the same place at the end of the novel to convey this shift in tone.

CHAPTER FIVE

Heading into the Blank Page

Activity Checklist

- [ ] Title Library
- [ ] Name Your Novel
- [ ] Make a Noveling Plan of Action
- [ ] Break the Blank-Page Barrier
- [ ] High Five!
- [ ] Kick in the Pants

This is the final chapter in your journaling adventure. You're just a few pages away from starting the book you've been threatening to write all these years. We suggest that you savor these final moments before you begin. Enjoy a few more hours watching TV. Look around at your clean and uncluttered home. Let your friends and family know how much you love them, because soon you will be sailing on the sea of your prolific prose.

We've heard that the cell phone reception at sea is pretty spotty.

This last section will help you get all your noveling ducks in a row before you set sail. We'll help you name your book, guide you into the first chapter of its life, and give you a time-management tool to keep your book/life/work balance in check. And right before we send you on your way, we'll give you a pep talk, a high five, and a strong kick in the pants.

Literally.

THE PRE-NOVELING CHECKLIST

Here's your final to-do list before you start writing your book:

1. **Name your novel.** Choosing a few words to encapsulate thousands and thousands of words is no easy task. The thing to keep in mind is that the title you choose now may change again and again as you write. That said, it's a good idea to start with a working title so you have something better to mention than My Novel while mingling with the literary cognoscenti. If you're titleless, we'll have you looking to your home library, then to your novel's core and pitch for inspiration. For example, if the core of your novel is "Only the good die young," and your pitch is "A rebel gone good for his high school sweetheart is given a chance to return to his wild rock-and-roll ways—a choice that might just save his life," then perhaps a good working title would be Live Long and Rock Out.

2. **Make a noveling plan of action.** As the staff of National Novel Writing Month, we're duty-bound to encourage you to throw caution to the wind, lock your Inner Editor in a dark cell, and write your first draft in thirty days. We also acknowledge (grudgingly) that there are other ways to write a novel. But no matter if you write your book in a month, in three months, or during the course of a year, we wholeheartedly believe that you need to set a firm deadline for yourself and follow a regular writing schedule.

3. **Break the blank-page barrier.** We know that starting a book is intimidating and that sloughing off the initial fear of getting it all wrong is easier said than done. If you and the blank page find yourself in a staring contest, we have an activity to get you past the paralyzing fear of putting pen to paper (or fingers to keyboard). We'll have you try out a series of different beginnings until you find the one that fits.

TITLE LIBRARY

It's probably safe to say that each book on your shelf has a title that was approved by a gang of supersmart people, including agents, editors, and publishers. That means your bookshelf is a great place to look for inspiration. Choose up to six books with titles you especially like, and write a couple of sentences about how each title relates to the book and/or why you think the author chose it. Does it refer to a setting, character, or plot point? Does it refer to a line in the book? Is it long? Short? Symbolic? Funny? Punny? Literal? Obvious?

TITLE

RELATIONSHIP TO TITLE

NOW that you have an idea of the way other writers have titled their works, it's your turn.

NAME YOUR NOVEL

 ACTIVITY

In the spaces below, write as many title ideas as you can muster. Things to refer to as you compile this list: the previous activity, your story's core (page 78), your novel's pitch (page 80), and the Playground (page 118—you may have written some great one-liners back there). If you already have a title, we suggest you do this activity anyway . . . you may find an even better title floating around in that gray matter of yours.

TITLE:

TITLE:

TITLE:

TITLE:

TITLE:

TITLE:

TITLE:

TITLE:

TITLE:

TITLE:

NOW Grab your favorite pen and write your title in the space provided on the inside front cover of this journal. Then do a jig.

In the Final Deadline box below, write a challenging yet attainable due date for your book. Between now and your final deadline, set ten mini-goals for yourself with corresponding rewards. For example, your first mini-goal could be completing chapters 1 through 3 with the award of a ninety-minute massage or an entire chocolate cake. Once you fill out the chart, we encourage you to buy or create a calendar (day planner, wall calendar, digital calendar) just for your Noveling Plan of Action. Put your final deadline and all your mini-goals on this calendar along with your detailed writing schedule. If you feel that it's helpful, share this calendar with your family and friends. That way you'll have people to hold you accountable and, if they're awesome friends and family, buy you gifts when you reach your mini-goals.

FINAL DEADLINE

MINI-GOAL	DUE DATE	REWARD
1.		
2.		
3.		
4.		
5.		
6.		
7.		
8.		
9.		
10.		

BREAK THE BLANK-PAGE BARRIER

If you did the Setting: Before & After activity in the previous chapter (page 100), you may already have a beginning that you like. If you're still not sure how to start, here's a list of writing prompts to get you past the blank-page blues. Write from as many of these prompts as you like in the following pages:

Start at the end. Give your readers a taste of what's in store to create intrigue.

Start at the Light the Fuse moment. Nothing like starting at the moment your story really takes off.

Start at the very, very, very beginning. Starting at birth and working to the present is a great way to build up a character in the beginning of your book.

Start with your core as the first sentence. Trust us on this one. "Aliens are jerks" is an awesome first line, right?

Start with a conflict between characters. Conflict is always interesting to read about. Why not suck your readers in with a little drama?

. . . .

TIP: The best advice we can give you as you start your book is not to overthink it. This is a rough draft, and you can go back anytime and strike your first sentence, opening page, and even the entire first chapter.

KEEP
GOING

KEEP
GOING

NOW Put this aside to revisit in a day or so. Then choose the beginning that gets you the most pumped to write the rest of your novel.

Congratulations, you did it! You completed this journal and now you're ready to write a book. You deserve a huge high five. And since novel writing can get lonely, this high five is here to be your best writing buddy. Come back and high five this page to celebrate all your noveling triumphs! And we also believe that the more high fives you give, the more plot bits from the universe you'll receive.

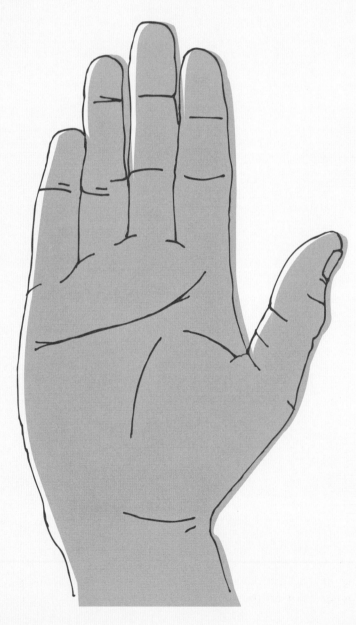

KICK IN
THE PANTS

OK, enough with the celebrating. It's time to get to work! To help with this, we're giving you this kick in the pants in addition to the high five. Turn to this page anytime you're in need of a good old-fashioned pants kicking. Reasons for the kicking may include any or all of the following: procrastination lasting more than forty-eight hours, a new addiction to B movies, writer's block, the "giving up seems like a good idea" syndrome, and so on.

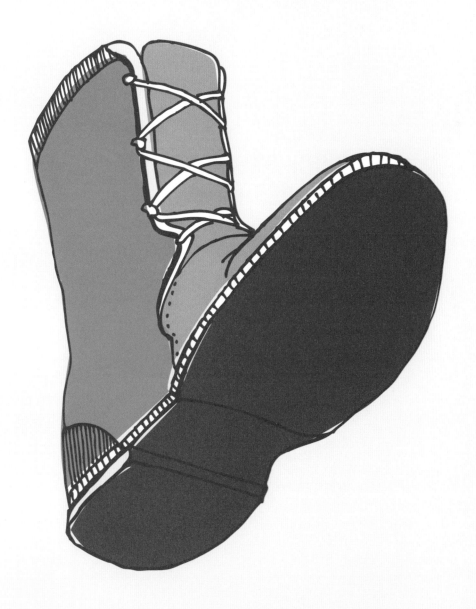

A QUICK PRE-NOVELING PEP TALK

OK. The journal is almost full, and the wheels are turning. Before you head off to meet that great-looking novel we mentioned in the introduction, we wanted to share a few things we've learned from wrestling with our own novel drafts over the years.

1. It's OK if your prose is less than dazzling on the first draft! Getting a beginning, middle, and end down on paper is much more important than writing pretty sentences. Write now. Polish later.

2. There will be times when you love your book so much that all you'll want to do is write.

3. There will be times when your book seems like such a disaster that all you'll want to do is shred it for hamster bedding.

4. If you just keep putting words on the page, you'll soon be in love again.

And you know what? The hardest part is behind you. Your story is here. Your characters are waiting. It's time for the next phase of this bookish adventure to begin.

You ready? You're set. Let's novel.

PLAYGROUND

You can use the following blank pages in whatever way you'd like. Write down overheard dialogue, key plot revelations, random facts about your main character's mother, more sensory-driven setting descriptions, your villain's grocery list, a day's worth of tweets from a supporting character, and so on. In case you need a little help, we've included a bunch of prompts to get you going. These pages need your words just like the world needs your novel!

Have each character retell his or her very first memory.

Read the phone book for great name ideas.

Write your opening scene from the point of view of your supporting character.

Write a scene of dialogue between your main character and a younger version of himself.

Read the pep talks from beloved authors at nanowrimo.org/pep.

Describe the worst thing that ever happened to your villain.

Flash forward twenty years into the future and write a scene that involves at least three of your characters.

Have your characters share tales of their first kisses.

Write about the last five things your main character bought and where she bought them.

Write a scene in which your protagonist and villain get drunk together.

Lock a few of your characters in a broken elevator.

People rarely get sick in novels. Have your protagonist come down with something.

Write a thank-you card from your protagonist to his sidekick.

Relate the dream your villain had last night.

Your protagonist's mother is interviewed for the local paper about her child's achievements. Write that article.

Add a scene in which your character loses something very valuable.

Write a week's worth of Facebook posts from a supporting character.
Take it a step further and add comments made by his friends . . . and enemies.

Have your villain bust out her high school yearbook. Write some of the notes she finds in it.

Have your character recount a (hilarious) childhood trauma.

Read the "Missed Connections" section of Craigslist for your town (or the setting of your novel).

Write a scene describing the way your main character's parents met.

Does your main character collect anything? Maybe he should.
Describe his collection and why he started it.

Write a really cheesy love song that your main character will sing to his love interest.

Describe the worst thing your main character ever did.

Write a scene in which your main character and the villain have to work together, and explain why.

Send your protagonist to a psychic. What does she find out?

Write a description of your setting in the style of a travel brochure.

Deprive a character of sleep for three days and write about how it affects him.

Read "Today's Featured Article" on Wikipedia and integrate something you learn into your novel.

Your main character finds a genie in a bottle. What three wishes does he make?

Place a few characters in a karaoke bar. Describe the scene and what songs they choose to sing.

Have a character win a huge prize out of the blue. How does she react when she gets the news?

Your villain hosts a dinner party. What's on the menu? Who is invited?

Write a 200-word newspaper obituary for your villain.

PROCRASTINATION STATION

We believe that one of the best ways to become a world-renowned author is by coloring famous novelists from the past. This activity builds character and hones skills such as procrastination and crayon sharpening. Come back to these pages whenever your brain needs a little break from all that thinking.

GUSTAVE FLAUBERT
1821–1880

JANE AUSTEN
1775–1817

MARY SHELLEY
1797–1851

FYODOR DOSTOYEVSKY
1821–1881

CHRIS BATY founded National Novel Writing Month (NaNoWriMo) in 1999, overseeing its growth from 21 San Francisco Bay Area participants to more than 200,000 writers in ninety countries. Chris is an award-winning writer, twelve-time NaNoWriMo winner, and the author of *No Plot? No Problem! A Low-Stress, High-Velocity Guide to Writing a Novel in 30 Days,* and *The No Plot? No Problem! Novel-Writing Kit.*

LINDSEY GRANT is the program director for National Novel Writing Month. She has written three novels during her time with NaNoWriMo. She holds an MFA in creative nonfiction and English from Mills College in Oakland, California.

TAVIA STEWART-STREIT received her BA in creative writing from the University of Southern California. She is currently the operations manager at the Office of Letters and Light. In addition, she is the founder and executive director of Invisible City Audio Tours. Tavia is a coauthor of National Novel Writing Month's *Young Novelist Workbook* and Script Frenzy's *Young Scriptwriter Workbook,* and her fiction has been published in the literary journals *Smokelong Quarterly, Spark,* and *We Still Like.*

ACKNOWLEDGMENTS

The authors wish to thank the staff and board of the Office of Letters and Light, the participants and municipal liaisons of NaNoWriMo and Script Frenzy, Jen Arzt, Steve Baker, Martha Baty, Pat Bowen, Becca Cohen, Arielle Eckstut, Lindsay Edgecombe, Penny and Rick Ellis, Jim and Linda Grant, Daniel Greenberg, Jennifer Kong, Michael Morris, Ashley Nickels, Katie "Kathy" O'Neill, Peet's Coffee, Mirrin Reagan, John Sanders, William Kent Stewart, John Stewart-Streit, Erin Thacker, and Karen and Bill White.

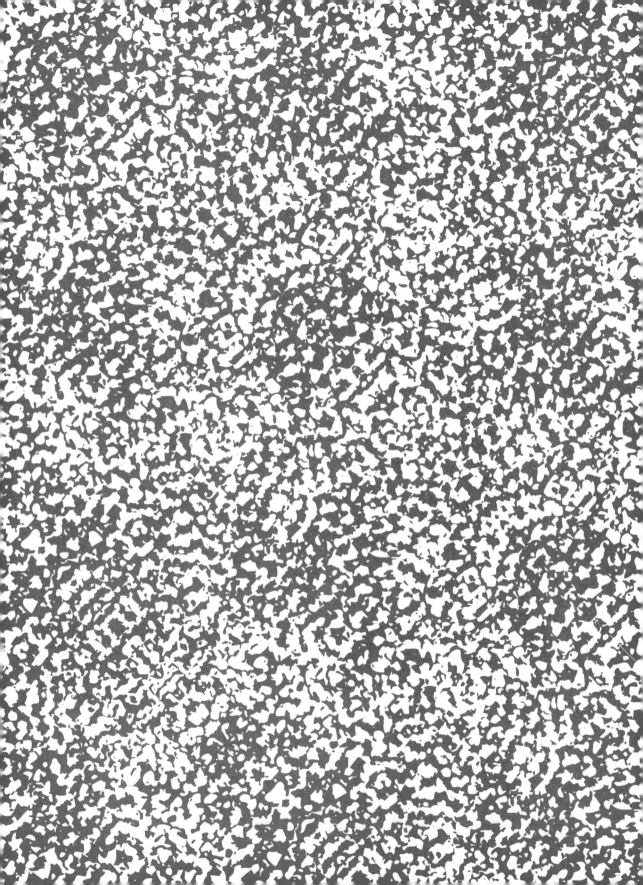

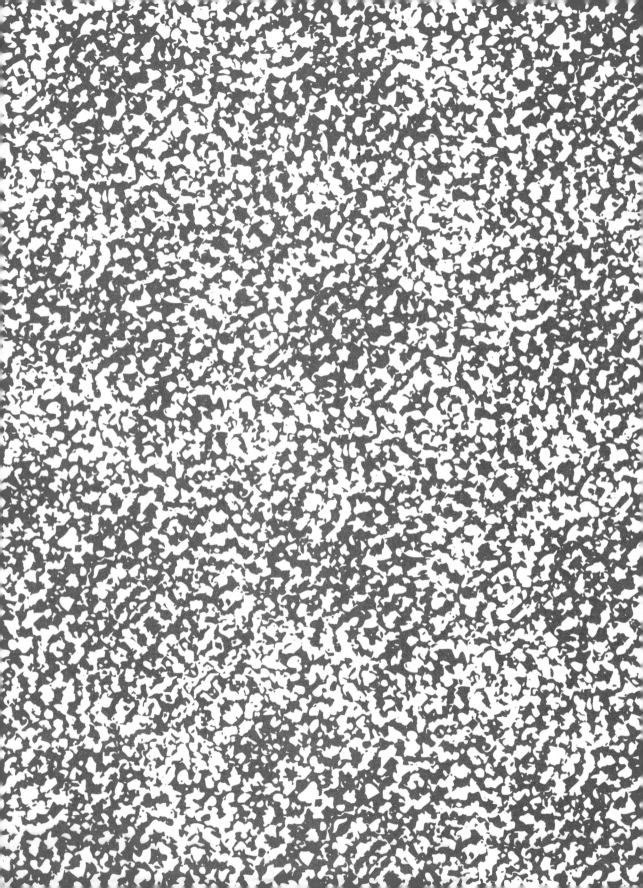